Mykonos
Travel Guide

Quick Trips Series

No part of this publication may be reproduced, stored in a retrieval system, or transmitted, in any form or by any means without the prior written permission of the publisher, nor be otherwise circulated in any form of binding or cover other than that in which it is published and without similar condition being imposed on the subsequent purchaser. If there are any errors or omissions in copyright acknowledgements the publisher will be pleased to insert the appropriate acknowledgement in any subsequent printing of this publication. Although we have taken all reasonable care in researching this book we make no warranty about the accuracy or completeness of its content and disclaim all liability arising from its use.

Copyright © 2016, Astute Press
All Rights Reserved.

Table of Contents

MYKONOS — 5
- 🌐 CUSTOMS & CULTURE 7
- 🌐 GEOGRAPHY 9
- 🌐 WEATHER & BEST TIME TO VISIT 10

SIGHTS & ACTIVITIES: WHAT TO SEE & DO — 13
- 🌐 MYKONOS TOWN 13
- 🌐 ANO MERA TOWN 16
- 🌐 LITTLE VENICE 18
- 🌐 WINDMILLS 19
- 🌐 PETROS THE PELICAN 21
- 🌐 PARAPORTIANI CHURCH 22
- 🌐 DELOS ISLAND & ANCIENT RUINS 24
- 🌐 ARMENISTIS LIGHTHOUSE 27
- 🌐 HORA PIRATE ALLEYWAYS 27
- 🌐 NIGHTCLUBS 29
- 🌐 THE HOTTEST BEACH: PSAROU 31
- 🌐 MORE EXCELLENT BEACHES 33

BUDGET TIPS — 36
- 🌐 ACCOMMODATION 36

Morfoulas Studios	36
Hotel Milena	37
Madalena Hotel	37
🌐 **PLACES TO EAT**	**38**
Antonini's	38
Casa di Giorgio	39
Kiki's Tavern	40
Philippi	41
🌐 **SHOPPING**	**41**
Soho-Soho	42
Nikoletta	42
Skaropoulos	43
Scala II Gallery	43

KNOW BEFORE YOU GO 45

🌐 **ENTRY REQUIREMENTS**	**45**
🌐 **HEALTH INSURANCE**	**46**
🌐 **TRAVELLING WITH PETS**	**46**
🌐 **AIRPORTS**	**47**
🌐 **AIRLINES**	**48**
🌐 **CURRENCY**	**49**
🌐 **BANKING & ATMS**	**49**
🌐 **CREDIT CARDS**	**50**
🌐 **RECLAIMING VAT**	**50**
🌐 **TIPPING POLICY**	**51**
🌐 **MOBILE PHONES**	**52**
🌐 **DIALLING CODE**	**53**
🌐 **EMERGENCY NUMBERS**	**53**
🌐 **PUBLIC HOLIDAYS**	**53**
🌐 **TIME ZONE**	**54**

- Daylight Savings Time 54
- School Holidays 55
- Trading Hours 55
- Driving Laws 55
- Smoking Laws 56
- Drinking Laws 57
- Electricity 57
- Tourist Information (TI) 57
- Food & Drink 58
- Websites 59

MYKONOS TRAVEL GUIDE

Mykonos

Look over the Aegean Sea from the top of one of the bleached-white buildings of Mykonos. The homes and churches of this exotic Greek island appear to cascade down the hillside into the sea which then converges with the sky in a mixture of beautiful blue.

MYKONOS TRAVEL GUIDE

Church bells ring softly, and nearby a Vespa motorbike buzzes its way past you, on the way to a long lunch, or a family visit on a lazy Sunday.

Mykonos is an island for the senses. Freshly-sautéed calamari reaches your nose before it reaches your mouth, the garlic and oil letting your taste buds know that they are in for a treat. Light, crisp wine bubbles in the glass as you relax after a long day touring, or just lounging on the beach. At night, that lazy mellow day slowly morphs into an island-wide party, as Mykonos welcomes revelers from all parts of the world to party in its famous nightclubs all night long.

Mykonos has not always been quite so conducive to long mellow vacation days and happy nights. In fact, Greek mythology asserts that this very island was the location of

MYKONOS TRAVEL GUIDE

the war between Zeus, King of the Gods, and the Titans, the huge and violent children of the Gods. However, the war fortunately did not last forever, and the island was named after a child of Apollo, God of music and poetry. It is that tradition that gained traction in Mykonos, winning over its violent history, and this island has been a get-away, first for the Greeks, then for the entire world, since the times of Ancient Greece.

Since the 1950's the island has been an extremely popular tourist destination, and along with Santorini, is probably the most visited and the most popular destination of the Greek Islands. There is a little something for everyone here, and expect long, luxurious days on the beach and long, vibrant nights out on the town, where you'll find locals and tourists hailing from all

MYKONOS TRAVEL GUIDE

over the globe participating in the Island's all-night dance parties.

For a visit as cultural as it is historical, as fun as it is relaxing, Mykonos will not disappoint. Here, you will find the sun shining more than it is not, and the locals smiling and welcoming, no matter the time of day.

🌍 Customs & Culture

Mykonos is a Greek Island, and although the official language is Greek, you'll find that because of the great many tourists who visit the island each year, most of the individuals who cater to the tourism industry will speak English with no difficulty. If you find that you'd like to get away from the other tourists for a while, it's a good idea to head inland, to Ano Mera, a small town that is a few kilometers inland from Mykonos. Here, you will enjoy a

MYKONOS TRAVEL GUIDE

quiet afternoon in the shadow of its church, built in the 16th century, and a bright reminder of the strong Catholic tradition of Greece.

Mykonos has a vibrant culture that has had a variety of influences over the course of history. An important island for Ancient Greece, the island then fell under Venetian rule, and then taken over by the Turks, who bought and sold the residents of the islands as slaves, until Greece won its independence in 1830. Even after this time, the area continued to be besieged by foreigners, this time by pirates, and the island only fell back into tourism in the middle of the 20th century.

This time, the foreigners don't come to enslave or pillage the local population, rather to share in the local food and drink and carve out a small space of beach to relax in.

MYKONOS TRAVEL GUIDE

You will find the population of Mykonos extremely relaxed and open-minded, notwithstanding its more traditional roots. It is considered one of the premier destinations for gay tourists in the Mediterranean. Go for the sun, go for the dancing, go for the food, or the ancient history. In any case, you will be amazed.

🌍 Geography

Mykonos lies in the South Aegean Sea, and is a small island, taking up an area of only around 86 square kilometers. To get here, you have a couple options: by air or by sea. Mykonos Island National Airport is only around 4 kilometers from Mykonos City, and has connections from many cities in Europe and Greece. You can choose to catch a taxi from the airport to your destination which will cost no more than about 10 Euros, or check to see if your hotel or hostel offers a shuttle from

MYKONOS TRAVEL GUIDE

the airport. There is no public transportation (bus or train) from the airport.

Also, you can choose to take a ferry from neighboring islands. This is a relatively cheap and convenient way to arrive to the island, and a wonderful way to take in the gorgeous Greek seas and the approaching white buildings on the coast of the island as you come into port. You can go to this website to check schedules and fares: http://www.ferries.gr/greek-islands-ferry/ferry_mykonos.htm

🌎 Weather & Best Time to Visit

It is not a surprise that visitors choose to come to this island most of the year. The summers are warm, and sometimes hot (especially July and August), and the

MYKONOS TRAVEL GUIDE

winters are crisp and cool, but rarely dipping below 50 degrees Fahrenheit.

You will find the most tourists in May, June, July and August, where people flood the island from other areas of Greece, Europe, and North America. This is when the clubs are open and most people are here for the party scene. Also, you will find the most local visitors around Pentecost, when many Greeks come to the island for that holy weekend.

There is a bit of a rainy season in February and March, but even in these "wetter" months, it hardly ever rains for the entire day. It's safe to say that no matter when you visit this island, you will find some stores open, and the beaches white and welcoming, but if you're here for the night scene, you may not want to come October – March,

MYKONOS TRAVEL GUIDE

when most of the revelers have gone home, and clubs have closed their stores for the winter.

Before coming to the island, it's a good idea to check the websites of the clubs and restaurants listed below to get a sense for what is open, and when. Most of the websites are very informative, and some have contact forms you can use to contact management directly for any specific questions about when you're coming to the island.

MYKONOS TRAVEL GUIDE

MYKONOS TRAVEL GUIDE

Sights & Activities: What to See & Do

🌑 Mykonos Town

Mykonos Town (also known as Hora) is the busiest town of the island, and is where most of the part-scene is happening. What is especially beautiful about this town is that even though there is a modern "feel" to the town, with the beachwear both on and off the beach, and the all-night dance parties, it has also maintained an authentic atmosphere the buildings still constructed in the local Cycladic manner (clean, white lines and short, compact houses and villas).

Mykonos is a veritable maze of shops, alleyways, small passageways, and restaurants, all clustered around a main harbor. The main harbor, also known as the Great Harbor, is where you'll be able to get the ferries on and off

MYKONOS TRAVEL GUIDE

the island, and is also a great photography opportunity at the end of the day, when the fishermen off-load their daily catches to bring into the restaurants to be stewed, sautéed, or fried for that evening's offering.

One of the beaches you can walk to from the town itself is Megali Ammos, which is only a short walk, so you won't have to hassle with transportation there and back. It is not one of the most popular beaches, as it doesn't offer the stunning view and fine, white sand of the other beaches on the island, but is a great place to get away from the crowds and mellow out for the day. If you find yourself sunning yourself all day has made you hungry Joanna's Niko's Taverna is a restaurant with inexpensive food and is right on the beach.

MYKONOS TRAVEL GUIDE

Once you've wandered through the town, or soaked up enough sun, why not do what you came here for: party the night away! Keep in mind that to drinks in Mykonos is fairly costly; but you can always hit up the supermarket during the day to buy a cheap bottle of wine and start the night out in your hotel before you head out for the evening. In fact, most of the club scene only begins late in the evening: after 11 or 12, and lasts into the dawn, so you'll find most locals will do the same: stay at dinner late, go home for some after dinner drinks, and then head out to the town after freshening up a bit.

Before the night on the town, make the most of the long, sunny days and sit outside for sunset, alongside the other tourists as well as most of the locals. You may want to head to Caprice, with its cave-like interior lit with candles and the porch outside. It is not too big, so if you're

MYKONOS TRAVEL GUIDE

heading there, best do so early enough to catch a chair outside, or to get one of the cozy tables inside, to gaze out the windows at the Aegean Sea. This is a place where the locals go to catch the sunset, and you'll find it crowded, but not for too long, as rarely do people stay for beyond the sunset. The view is spectacular: you'll be able to see the windmills, Little Venice, and of course the beautiful sea.

After your sunset drink, you may want to head to Matoyanni Street, where Aroma bar is an extremely popular place to go for after-dinner lounging and dancing. If you're rather into chilling out after a long day of relaxing on the beach and catching a movie, go to Cine Manto which is found in the Municipal Garden of Meletopoulou. Each night a film shows at about 9:00, and most are American films. The foreign films have English subtitles.

MYKONOS TRAVEL GUIDE

You will find in Mykonos that the buildings, bars, restaurants, and clubs are literally right on top one another, stacked up the hill around the harbor. If one place looks too busy, head up the road to another, and come back later. Chances are you won't have a boring night here during party season. In the off-season many of the clubs will be closed, but the locals will be around and some shops and restaurants will be open. So if it's a sleepy scene you're after, avoid those hot summer nights, and come visit Mykonos in the off-season.

🌐 Ano Mera Town

A few kilometers inland from Mykonos Town, you'll find a charming city far away from the hustle and bustle of her coastal sister. In contrast to the sheen of glittery Mykonos, you'll find Ano Mera a bit unapologetically

MYKONOS TRAVEL GUIDE

dusty, with a quiet town center and square. On the square, you'll find a produce market that also sells excellent local cheese and bread, and makes for a lovely Sunday morning stroll. The market is mostly open only on Sundays, but on the days it is closed, you won't have any trouble finding a bakery or butcher to help you put together a sandwich for lunch.

You will want to visit The Monastery of Panagia Tourliani, which was built in the 1700's, and is really the village's only landmark. The altar was made in Florence in the Baroque style and is adorned with some beautiful gold-leaf decorations. Keep in mind that you need an appointment to visit. Call (0289/71249) to make a reservation, best done before your visit in case many people have also called for appointments. After your visit, head down to the tavern directly across the street and enjoy a long, lazy lunch.

To get to Ano Mera, take a very short bus trip from Mykonos Town. Ano Mera is only a few kilometers away from Mykonos, but because of the hills, you'll want to ride instead of walk. There is only one road from Mykonos Town to Ano Mera, so if you're driving your own vehicle, you will have no problems finding this quaint Greek village.

🌐 Little Venice

Little Venice epitomizes the beauty of the Greek Islands. This neighborhood developed from the stunning Alevkantra beach, and is considered one of the most romantic places in all of Mykonos. The neighborhood is filled to the brim with quaint little houses, almost

Maganos Apartments

Maganos apartments are a very nice choice for your vacations as it provides with multiple living choices.

Choose double or triple room with the view of Aegean's deep blue that make you peaceful and travel enjoying the Greek blue sky.

Our are full equipped with the essential appliances which offer you convenience and functionality for a pleasant stay.

Our apartments have double rooms and are able to accommodate up to five people. It's the perfect solution for peaceful vacation with enough places for the family and company.

The opulent breakfast is based on Mediterranean and Greek cuisine by the pool with a view to Agia Anna's bay that will contribute to have a dynamic start of your day.

Maganos apartments' location except of the magnificent view combines calmness and easy access to Agia Anna, Paraga and Platys Gialos beaches.

Furthermore they are pretty close to the famous Paradise beach. Maganos Apartments is a family business and that's what it offers you, family and tranquil environment ideal for unforgettable vacation.

Agia Anna, Mykonos 84600
Tel.: +30 22890 24644. Mob.: +30 6932 815687
info@maganosapartments.gr

MYKONOS TRAVEL GUIDE

dangerously balancing on the edge of the Aegean. If it's a sunset unlike you've never seen before that you're after, then head down to Little Venice at the end of the day – those whitewashed buildings set against the deep blue of the sea is a scene straight from a picture postcard. You'll find yourself taking more than just a few photos.

Here you can stay in a boutique hotel, or even if you're willing to fork out just a couple hundred more Euros, stay in a tiny little fisherman's hut right at the edge of the sea. You may need to do a little digging to find out who is renting out his hut, and when, so your best option is to book a night or two in a hotel or bed and breakfast before your arrival, then check with your hotel about what huts are being rented that week.

MYKONOS TRAVEL GUIDE

But if you're just in the neighborhood for the evening, you won't be bored. Check out the art galleries, many of which frequently display works from famous artists (many of whom love to visit this neighborhood), and then head to one of the converted fishing huts near the sea for dinner or dancing. The best thing about eating in one of the fishing huts is not just its proximity to the sea and cozy accommodations, but also knowing that the seafood you're eating probably came from the sea a mere few hours before.

Little Venice is now considered one of the most-photographed neighborhoods in all of Europe, and once you visit, when you're on your third or fourth roll of film, you'll understand why.

MYKONOS TRAVEL GUIDE

🌐 Windmills

While many of us liken windmills to the windy flats of the Netherlands, you may be surprised to learn that some of the most picturesque windmills can actually be found right on the island of Mykonos. These 16 windmills, many of them constructed by the Venetians in the 1500's, were mainly used to grind wheat, which was an important staple in both the diet and economy of the people of Mykonos. Five of them rest on the hill above Mykonos Town, and are visible from any area of the town, and were actually in operation until only about 50 years ago. Up until they ceased production, they were a significant income source for residents, many of whom now rely on the tourism trade for that income.

Unlike the windmills farther north in Holland, these windmills, as is the Greek Island tradition, are all whitewashed, and all have a pointed roof. This is the type of windmill that can be found in the other Cyclades Islands around Mykonos.

For a great view of sunset, head to one of the five windmills up the hill from Mykonos, and watch as the sun turns the whitewashed walls pink, orange, and yellow as it sets. It's an absolutely stunning photo opportunity. They are impossible to miss: they are visible in any point in Mykonos.

🌐 Petros the Pelican

This is a very charming story, and a testament to the small-town feel of Mykonos, even though tourists seem to take over the island for the summer each year. In 1958, a fisherman brought in a wounded pelican and nursed him back to health. The pelican made himself right at home,

MYKONOS TRAVEL GUIDE

and the entire town of Mykonos made sure his needs were taken care of, each and every day. For some reason, the pelican refused to ever leave the island again, earning his place as the mascot of the entire island. The residents named him "Petros", which means "rock", assumedly referring to his stubborn attitude towards moving off the island.

One day, sadly, Petros died from being hit by a car almost 30 years after he had been brought to the island, and residents and tourists alike were surprised to learn how much an important part of their everyday culture he had become. Therefore, the townspeople bought three more pelicans, one named "Petros" (the second), and when you visit Mykonos today, chances are you'll see one of these new pelicans out and about, also stubbornly refusing to leave the island. If you were those pelicans, would you do any differently? Feel free to take pictures, but the locals tend to be quite protective over these special birds, so try not to get too close as to scare them away!

🌑 Paraportiani Church

Main Harbor of Mykonos Town

Paraportiani is also a must-see in Mykonos Town. It seems like a quintessential Greek church in both design and color, even though it is not: it is actually a mixture of four styles, including Byzantine and "Vernacular", or more casual, styles. It is one of the most photographed all the churches on the Greek islands, and it's not hard to see why. The white walls against the blue summer sky is an absolutely stunning contrast.

MYKONOS TRAVEL GUIDE

The church was built in the 1450's, and was originally situated next to the now destroyed medieval castle in Mykonos. The building actually consists of 4 different temples situated around one main church. The churches around the main church are: Aghios Sozontas, Aghii Anargyri, Aghia Anastasia, and Aghios Efstathios, and this entire structure is what is referred to as the Paraportiani. The entire structure is beautifully engineered, with a central dome uniting all its parts.

The church would be a beautiful stop on your way to Little Venice to catch the sunset; it is right in the "Castle District", or the oldest district in Mykonos, and right on the way from the center of Mykonos down into Little Venice. The church was actually directly next to the large medieval castle that once stood in this area, although unfortunately it has long since deteriorated and disappeared.

All of Mykonos town is so compact that it is hard to miss landmarks such as Paraportiani, but if you do find yourself a little turned-around, just ask any shopkeeper, and he or she will point you in the right direction.

Address: Ayion Anargyron, Little Venice, Mykonos

🌍 Delos Island & Ancient Ruins

You simply can't come to Greece and miss the opportunity to see some Greek ruins. It's fascinating to see how long people have lived on this island, and imagine how much the island has changed since people started inhabiting it. Delos is legally a part of Mykonos because of its proximity to Mykonos, and it's a short boat

MYKONOS TRAVEL GUIDE

ride to the island. Excavations have found huts, and proof of human life, on the island since the 3rd Millenium BC, and Greek mythology have the gods Apollo and Artemis being born on this island.

The island of Delos was even mentioned in the Greek Odyssey, and has had historical significance for many civilizations, although it seems that the last people to build here left with the ancient Greeks. This could be because of the sacred nature of the island; it has gone through dozens of "purification" processes during its tenure as the birthplace of Gods, and also as the location of several important temples in which to worship those Gods. You'd be hard-pressed to find such culturally significant ruins as there are here.

MYKONOS TRAVEL GUIDE

There are extensive excavations going on in Delos, and have been for quite some time, so it is an extremely interesting place to visit to both see the ruins that have already been excavated, and also the archaeologists at work. According to a recent census, the population of Delos is only 14 individuals, but you will find many more come to visit this historically-significant island.

Some sights to see while you're here include:

- The Minoan Fountain, built before the 5th century, BC

- Several of the town's former market squares, with its beautiful statues and columns

MYKONOS TRAVEL GUIDE

- The Temple of the Delians, dedicated to Apollo, with its Doric columns

- The statue to Dionysus, erected around 300 BC, built next to the theater

- The Temple of Isis

- The House of Dionysus – this was actually a private house that has beautifully crafted mosaics, one of the God Dionysus.

The boats for Delos leave from Hora in Mykonos, and there are several options of ferry companies. They all cost about the same. The trip will cost less than 9 Euro round-trip, and takes around 30 minutes one-way. For more information, go to this website for updated ferry times: http://www.mykonos-accommodation.com/

🌐 Armenistis Lighthouse

Another worthwhile on your trip in Mykonos is the Armenistis Lighthouse, particularly of the view of all the boats arriving and departing from Mykonos. This is probably one of the youngest of the Mykonos landmarks, as it was built at the end of the 19th century. It is worth going to for the view, and for the beautiful architecture.

It is a bit of an adventure to get there, and you may have to speak to your hotel or hostel for transportation options, as there is only one road up there from the village of Agios Stephanos. But it's well worth the drive along the cliffs of Mykonos, the Aegean Sea glistening in the background.

MYKONOS TRAVEL GUIDE

🌎 Hora Pirate Alleyways

With all the layers of history found on Mykonos, it should come as no surprise that Pirates also played a part in this island's history, threatening the local population with canons and swords, pillaging for wine and grain. In fact, you may notice that Hora, or the old part of Mykonos (Mykonos Town), is built in a series of corridors and alleyways, wrapping themselves around each other on the way back from the harbor.

These are named the 'Pirate Alleyways" because they were evidently meant to confuse the Maltese Pirates who would come ashore to pillage the town. Nowadays, these streets make for a fun night out among the restaurants, bars, and clubs of this area. You'll never have so much fun getting lost in your life.

MYKONOS TRAVEL GUIDE

For an experience not to miss, head to Koursaros Restaurant in Hora, which has craftily incorporated elements of a real pirate ship in its architecture. It has an absolutely beautiful garden to dine al fresco if the weather allows. Go for the view, and the ambience, but most of all, go for the freshest fish you will ever eat.

Address: Meletopoulou Square, Limni, Mykonos Town 84600, Mykonos

Telephone +30 22890 78140

http://www.koursarosmykonos.gr/

🌎 Nightclubs

Especially in the hot summer months, when the entire island seems to pulse with the rhythm of electronic music, it's hard to find a street without a nightclub on it. With so many options, it may be hard to choose. Here are some

MYKONOS TRAVEL GUIDE

of the best nightclubs in Mykonos, for you to make the best of both your days and your nights.

Want to go to the number 2 sexiest beach bar in the world (according to Travel Magazine)? Put on your skimpiest clothes and head down to Tropicana Beach Bar on the famous (and nude) Paradise Beach. After a day with no clothes on whatsoever, you can imagine how much clothing is on (or off) in this thumping club.

http://www.tropicanamykonos.com/

Space Dance is located right near the Great Harbor in the center of Mykonos Town, and is probably the most popular nightclub on the island. Expect a closing time of …never.

MYKONOS TRAVEL GUIDE

http://www.spacemykonos.com/

If you're in Mykonos during the non-peak season, then a good bet for some dancing action is the **Scandinavian Bar**, which has a good turn-out whatever night of the week.

http://www.skandinavianbar.com/

Cavo Paradiso is another famous club to check out while in Mykonos, and is in Paradise Bay. This may be closed during the off-season, so check the website before travelling. The attraction for this pulsating club is its pool and the stunning view over the Aegean Sea, as well as its rotating cast of international visiting DJ's that grace these walls.

MYKONOS TRAVEL GUIDE

Address: At Paradise Bay, on the left side of the Hill, Mikonos 846 00

Telephone: +30 22890 27205

www.cavoparadiso.gr

Finally, if you want to go party with your LGBT brothers and sisters, head to the oldest Gay Bar in Mykonos, which has been partying down for over 30 years. You'll find that this bar, Pierros, sometimes is so full that the party will spill over to a neighboring club, Mantos, where the music is just as loud and the crowd just as keen for a good time.

Address: Agias Kiriakis Square

🌍 The Hottest Beach: Psarou

With so many beaches to choose from in Mykonos, it may be downright impossible to choose the best one. There

MYKONOS TRAVEL GUIDE

are beaches for every type of body in any shape or size, clothed or not, bordering bars or bordering a serene cliff. A good idea is to ask at your accommodation for the best beach, as the locals have their secret places they might tell you if you ask nicely.

One of the most famous beaches is Psarou, at the resort of the same name. You'll find many of the locals have already rented a lounge chair and umbrella on this glistening-white shore, and that many of the lounge chairs fill up very quickly in the morning, particularly in peak season.

This beach is particularly popular with the locals because it is far away from other beaches that may have bars or nightclubs attached. Here the atmosphere is serene and relaxed (and clothing is not optional). Even if there is a waiting list to get a lounge chair, you probably could bribe the beach attendant with a few dollars. Don't be stingy. Paradise costs.

This beach is located about 4 kilometers away from Mykonos Town, near the Plati Gialos bus terminus, if you plan on taking a bus.

🌎 More Excellent Beaches

Paranga is a must-see for all travellers to Mykonos. The Aegean Sea doesn't get more beautiful than it does here, and you'll find this beach friendly for all sorts of travellers, including families. While here, you'll want to try **Tasos**, and want to try the local octopus dishes, as they were more than likely caught that very day.

MYKONOS TRAVEL GUIDE

If you have a car, then head down to **Fokos**, which is very secluded, and only approachable by a dirt road. Make sure you bought the insurance on the rental. There are no tourists here, no carefully dusted beach lounge chairs, and no hopping beach bars, just clean, unadulterated sand and sea. You can find a tiny "taverna" here, though, but don't expect a menu, only the freshest salads and seafood you could ever dream up.

If you're wanting to see a beautiful sunset, head to **Aghios Ioannis**, which is small, local, and also gives you the opportunity to view the fishermen bring in their catch at the end of each day. Follow those fishermen to the building they bring the fish to, and you'll find the restaurant you should spend the evening in.

MYKONOS TRAVEL GUIDE

Budget Tips

🌐 Accommodation

Mykonos offers options for just about anyone on any budget, but here are some great choices that will leave you with enough money for the all night parties.

Morfoulas Studios

Morfoulas Studios are located only steps away from the center of town, and is perched on a small hill overlooking the Sea. The building is absolutely beautifully constructed in the Cycladic design of clean lines and white paint. This is a great choice if you want a clean, relaxed Bed and Breakfast. Each room comes with a television and will have two or three twin beds. Expect to pay no more than about 50 Euros per night.

MYKONOS TRAVEL GUIDE

Morfoulas Studios

Despotika, Mykonos 846 00

Telephone: + 30 22890-23672

Hotel Milena

Hotel Milena is also an excellent budget choice, and boasts free breakfast and a free airport shuttle. It is in the Drafaki area, and is directly across from the bus stop to Mykonos Town. You can also choose to take the bus to Paradise and Paraga beaches. You will also find free WiFi in all the areas of the hotel. Hotel rooms average around 60 Euros per night.

Hotel Milena

Drafaki, Mykonos 846 00

Telephone: +30 22890-23126

http://www.hotelmilena.gr/

MYKONOS TRAVEL GUIDE

Madalena Hotel

If you're looking for the best of both worlds, then look no further than Madalena Hotel, which is located just one block away from Mykonos Town's city center, but high enough on a small hill that the hustle and bustle of the town below you can seem like miles away. It was recently renovated, and is decorated in the Cycladic style. Each room comes with free WiFi, and you can choose a sea view for a few extra Euros. As an added bonus, the property has a pool, if you can bear to tear yourself away from the Mykonos beach scene for an afternoon. All this for an average price of 34 Euros per night, and you'll want to book that extra weekend.

Madalena Hotel

Mykonos 846 00

MYKONOS TRAVEL GUIDE

Telephone: + 30 22890-28150

http://www.web-greece.gr/hotels/madalena/

🌐 Places to Eat

Antonini's

If you wind up in Mykonos during the off-season (not from November – March, when it's closed) and want the opportunity to rub elbows with the locals, then pop by Antonini's in Mykonos Town for some great stew, lamb, or many other local delicacies. If you're here during the peak-season, you'll wind up mostly eating with other tourists, but you won't find a better meal for under 20 Euros a person.

Antonini's

Plateia Manto, Hora

MYKONOS TRAVEL GUIDE

Telephone: +30 22890 22319

http://www.antoninimykonos.com/index%20en.html

Casa di Giorgio

Here's another story for you: Giorgio moved to Mykonos when he was just a young man, and decided to have a family here. He bought a charming house behind the Catholic cathedral, and settled in. A few years ago, his grandson decided to bring his grandfather's roots back to Mykonos, and established Casa di Giorgio, a fantastic Italian meal that you can enjoy for less than 20 Euro per person. Order the risotto or thin-crust pizza, or splurge for the shrimp (freshly brought in) pasta, and sit back and relax for an amazingly Italian evening in Greece.

Casa di Giorgio

1 Mitropoleos Street, Hora

MYKONOS TRAVEL GUIDE

Telephone: +20 69325 61998

http://casadigiorgio-mykonos.gr/

Kiki's Tavern

If you really want to get off the beaten path, then head to Kiki's Tavern at Atios Sostis Beach, in Ayios Sostis, Mykonos. So off the beaten path that it lacks electricity, this small tavern is only open until sundown, and doesn't even have a sign to announce its presence. You'll have to ask the locals or other more "in-the-know" tourists where to go. They serve unembellished, simple island food, grilled with little flair and very little money (Most entrees cost less than 15 Euros). Ask to eat in the courtyard, and enjoy the fresh salad or freshly grilled shrimp in the cool shade. It is a welcome oasis after a hot day on the beach.

MYKONOS TRAVEL GUIDE

Kiki's Tavern

Ayios Sostis Beach

Philippi

If you're in the mood for an inexpensive romantic night out, head to Philippi, which is actually located in a small garden in Mykonos Town. Indulge in their extensive wine list and enjoy the romantic and candlelit atmosphere in this tiny establishment. You won't spend more than 25 Euro a person, but you'll wind up spending an entire evening here with your loved one, soaking up the romantic atmosphere.

Philippi

Off Mayoyianni & Kaloyera streets

Telephone: +30 22890 22294

http://philippis.gr/garden%20rest%20bar.htm

🌐 Shopping

You don't have to look far and wide, particularly in peak season, to find a place to shop for souvenirs or those "just because" purchases in Mykonos. This town is as packed full of shops as it is places to eat and drink.

Soho-Soho

The most famous clothing store on the island has to be Soho-Soho, which has photographs of the stars when they shopped here (Tom Hanks being on that list), and you'll want to open your wallet wide for the fashion finds in this boutique.

Soho-Soho

81 Mayoyanni, Hora

Telephone: +20 22890 26760

http://www.sohosoho.gr/en/our_stores/

Nikoletta

For an interesting historical and cultural experience, hear to Nikoletta for some organic vegetable-dyed weavings that are handwoven and loomed by the residents of Mykonos, who were once known far and wide for this craft. This store is an amazing opportunity to see tradition that still holds fast, by the namesake craftswoman, Niki Xydaki.

Nikoletta

Telephone: + 30 22890 27503

Skaropoulos

If you favor shopping for the edible sorts of goodies, then head to Skaropoulos for award-winning pastries and confections that were even the favorite of Winston Churchill. It is family-owned, and Nikos and Frantzeska

Koukas are still cooking up family recipes such as their famous almond biscuits that you can eat there or take along for the journey.

Skaropoulos

Out of Mykonos Town, on the road to Ano Mera

Telephone: +2- 22890 24983

Scala II Gallery

You may want to bring some Greek art home with you, but want to take it home for a bargain. Head to Scala II Gallery for jewelry, painting, sculpture, and mixed-media arts, all by Greek artists, and all offered here at a discounted price. A bonus here is that the owner is also an owner of several apartments in Mykonos Town, so if you fancy an offbeat place to stay, best contact the gallery to see about availability.

MYKONOS TRAVEL GUIDE

Scala II Gallery

48 Mayoyianni, Hora

Telephone: +30 22890 26993

MYKONOS TRAVEL GUIDE

Know Before You Go

🌐 Entry Requirements

By virtue of the Schengen agreement, travellers from other countries in the European Union do not need a visa when visiting Greece. Additionally visitors from certain countries such as Canada, Japan, Israel, Australia, Argentina, Monaco, Andorra, Brazil, Brunei, Chile, Costa Rica, Croatia, Honduras, Guatemala, El Salvador, Nicaragua, Paraguay, Panama, San Marino, Singapore, South Korea, Uruguay, New Zealand and the Vatican State do not need visas if their stay in Greece does not exceed 90 days in a six month period. In the case of travellers from the USA, entry requirements will depend on the type of passport held. While visitors with a normal blue tourist passport will be able to enter the USA without a visa, holders of red official or black diplomatic passports must apply for a Schengen visa prior to departure and will face deportation if attempting to enter Greece without the necessary documentation.

🌐 Health Insurance

Citizens of other EU countries as well as residents from Switzerland, Norway, Iceland, Liechtenstein and the UK are covered for health care in Greece with the European Health Insurance Card (EHIC), which can be applied for free of charge. If you need a Schengen visa for your stay in Greece, you will also be required to obtain proof of health insurance for the duration of your stay (that offers at least €37,500 coverage), as part of your visa application. Visitors from Canada or the USA should check whether their regular health insurance covers travel and arrange for extended health insurance if required.

🌐 Travelling with Pets

Greece participates in the Pet Travel Scheme (PETS) which allows UK residents to travel with their pets without requiring quarantine upon re-entry. Pets travelling between different countries in the EU will need to be accompanied by a valid pet passport, which can be obtained from any licensed veterinarian in the EU. The animal will have to be microchipped and up to date on rabies vaccinations. To visit Greece, your pet will need to be accompanied by a good health certificate issued by a vet no more than ten days prior to your intended departure. The certificate must be in both English and Greek. You should also have a rabies vaccination certificate no less than 30 days and no

MYKONOS TRAVEL GUIDE

more than 12 months old. If travelling from a high rabies country, a blood titer test will need to be submitted three months prior to your travel plans. Your animal's microchip should be non-encrypted and compliant with a 15 digit ISO 11784/11785 number (or alternatively you will need to have your own scanner handy.) You will be required to make a declaration of non-commercial travel. If returning to the USA with a pet you adopted in Greece, your pet will need to be vaccinated against rabies at least 30 days prior to entry into the USA.

🌍 Airports

Athens International Airport (ATH) is the busiest airport in Greece. Located about 20km east of the city center, it is the main airport servicing Athens and the region of Attica. **Heraklion International Airport** (HER) is located on the island of Crete, about 5km east of the city of Heraklion. It is the second busiest airport in Greece. **Thessaloniki International Airport** (SKG), also known as Makedonia International Airport, provides access to Khalkidhiki, the region of Macedonia and the northern part of Greece. It is located in Mikra and serves Thessaloniki, the second largest city in Greece. **Rhodes International Airport** (RHO) is located on the western side of the island Rhodes. It is the 4th busiest airport in Greece, providing regular connections to Athens. **Corfu**

MYKONOS TRAVEL GUIDE

International Airport (CFU) is located on the island of Corfu, about 2km south of Corfu City. **Mykonos Island National Airport** (JMK) about 4km from Mykonos Town and **Santorini National Airport** (JTR), provide seasonal connections to the Cyclades at the peak of the summer holidays.

🌐 Airlines

Olympic Airlines, the national flag carrier of Greece for more than 50 years, ceased operation in 2009 due to bankruptcy. From the privatization of its assets, a regional airline, Olympic Air, was formed. Ellinair is a small Greek airline that was established in 2013 and provides regional connections between Athens and Thessaloniki as well as regular flights to Russia, Latvia and the Ukraine. Minoan Air is a small airline based in Heraklion on the island of Crete. It provides connections to Kos and Rhodes, as well as seasonal flights to Santorini and Mytilene. Sky Express is also headquartered in Crete and provides regional connections to 18 Greek destinations. Another Greek airline based in Crete, Bluebird Airways, flies to the Greek destinations of Araxos, Corfu, Kos and Rhodes as well as destinations in Israel, Russia and Turkey.

Athens International Airport serves as a main hub for Aegean Airlines as well as Olympic Air. Olympic Air also uses Rhodes International Airport as a secondary hub. Heraklion International Airport serves as a hub for Bluebird Airways

Minoan Air and Sky Express. It is also a focus city for Aegean Airlines. Thessaloniki International Airport serves as a hub for Aegean Airlines, Astra Airlines, Ellinair and Ryanair.

🌐 Currency

The currency of Greece is the Euro. It is issued in notes in denominations of €500, €200, €100, €50, €20, €10 and €5. Coins are issued in denominations of €2, €1, 50c, 20c, 10c, 5c, 2c and 1c.

🌐 Banking & ATMs

You will find ATMs in the larger centers of Greece, although smaller towns may only have a single ATM machine. Greek ATMs are configured for four-digit PIN numbers - make sure your card is compliant before leaving home. However, the financial crisis has introduced an added complication. While daily limits imposed on Greek citizens do not apply to tourists visiting the country, you may encounter ATMs that have run out of cash or banks that are reluctant to exchange pounds for euros. The limits imposed on Greeks will also make it difficult for shop owners to provide change for cash sales. To be on the safe side, consider taking cash in smaller denominations. Do remember to advise your bank of your travel plans before leaving home.

🌐 Credit Cards

The Credit Cards most widely used in Greece are MasterCard and Visa, although American Express is also accepted at more touristy centers. While shops and many hotels accept credit cards, most restaurant options will be limited to cash. Credit card machines in Greece are configured for chip-and-pin type credit cards and you may run into trouble with an older magnetic strip credit card. Greece also has representatives of Western Union, for international money transfers.

🌐 Reclaiming VAT

If you are not from the European Union, you can claim back VAT (Value Added Tax) paid on your purchases in Greece. The VAT rate in Greece is 23 percent, although it varies on certain types of goods and you will qualify for a refund on goods of €120 and over. To reclaim, you must ask the merchant to fill in a refund voucher. You will be asked to show your passport. Make sure that the form is completed and attach your sales slip to the form. The goods must be inspected at the place where you leave the European Union. Here, the necessary documentation will be processed. Your refund will only be valid for items that are still unused at your time of departure. If the merchant is affiliated to Global Refund or Premier Tax Free, you will be able to collect the refund from their offices at the airport in the currency of your choice. A 4 percent service charge will be levied. Alternatively, you could ask for a refund on your credit card or contact the retailer directly, once you have returned home.

Tipping Policy

At the hotel, tip the porter €1 per bag and the housekeeper €1 per day. At restaurants, you should tip between 5 and 10 percent of the bill, depending on its size. Bear in mind that the service or cover charge on your restaurant bill (usually around €1) is for the table's bread and water. It is customary to tip tour guides in Greece. For a group tour, between €2 and €5 per person is fair. For private tours, €20 per person is the expected rate. On a yacht cruise, tip the captain or skipper between 5 and 15 percent (in a closed envelope) for him to distribute amongst crew members. With taxi drivers, it is customary to round off the amount or to tip between 5 and 10 percent. If you employed a private driver, tip him €20 per day.

Mobile Phones

Most EU countries, including Greece uses the GSM mobile service. This means that most UK phones and some US and Canadian phones and mobile devices will work in Greece. However, phones using the CDMA network will not be compatible. While you could check with your service provider about coverage before you leave, using your own service in roaming mode will involve additional costs. The alternative is to purchase a Greek SIM card to use during your stay in Greece. Greece has three mobile networks. They are Cosmote, Vodafone and Wind. Of the three networks, Wind is the most economic, but offers the lowest coverage. With each network, you can choose between packages that offer data only or a mixture of voice, text and data. A basic Cosmote SIM with no credit can be purchased for €5, but you will want to look at some of the available package deals as well. Vodafone offers a starter package that includes 2 GB data that can be ordered online for €15, but will cost €20 in store. At Wind you have the choice of a free SIM with top-up cards from €10 or a SIM for €5. They also offer mobile broadband. As per legislation that came into effect in 2009, all Greek SIM cards must be registered before they can be activated. This can only be done in person and you will need to show some form of identification, such as a passport. You can recharge your airtime by buying scratch cards or electronically from ATMs, certain vendors or online with a debit or credit card.

🌏 Dialling Code

The international dialling code for Greece is +30.

MYKONOS TRAVEL GUIDE

🌐 Emergency numbers

General Emergencies: 112

Police: 100

Fire Brigade: 199

Emergency Medical Service: 166

Coast Guard: 108

Emergency Social Assistance: 197

Tourist Police: 171

MasterCard: 00 800 11 887 0303

Visa: 00 800 11 638 0304

🌐 Public Holidays

1 January: New Year's Day

6 January: Day of the Epiphany

February/March: Orthodox Ash Monday

25 March: Independence Day

April (variable): Orthodox Good Friday

April (variable): Orthodox Easter Sunday

April (variable): Orthodox Easter Monday

1 May: Labour Day

May/June: Orthodox Pentecost

May/June: Orthodox Whit Monday

15 August: Assumption Day

28 October: Ochi Day (Oxi Day/Ohi Day)

25 December: Christmas Day

26 December: Second Christmas Day

🌐 Time Zone

Greece falls in the Eastern European Time Zone. This can be calculated (from the end of October to the end of March) as follows: Greenwich Mean Time/Coordinated Universal Time (GMT/UTC) +2; Eastern Standard Time (North America) -6; Pacific Standard Time (North America) -9.

🌐 Daylight Savings Time

Clocks are set forward one hour on the last Sunday of March and set back one hour on the last Sunday of October for Daylight Savings Time.

🌐 School Holidays

The academic year begins in the second week of September and ends in mid June. The summer holiday is from mid June to the first third of September. There are short breaks between Christmas and New Year and also around Easter.

🌐 Trading Hours

In Greece, trading hours vary according to the type of business. You can expect supermarkets to be open from 8am to 8pm on weekdays and until 6pm on Saturdays. Most other shops are open between 9am and 1pm and then again for a late session between 6pm and 9pm. The hours from 1.30pm to 5.30pm are for lunch and siesta, especially in the summer months. Post Offices are open from 8am to 8pm on weekdays and from 8am to 2pm on Saturdays. Shops that cater for tourists may be open until 11pm, especially during the peak tourist season. Pharmacies conform to normal shopping hours, but are usually closed on Saturdays.

🌐 Driving Laws

Greeks drive on the right hand side of the road. A driver's licence from any of the European Union member countries is valid in Greece, but visitors from non-EU countries should apply for an International Driver's License. The minimum driving age in Greece is 18. You will need to have a Green Insurance certificate, also known as a Green Card to cover third party liability and your vehicle needs standard safety gear such as warning triangles, a first aid kit and fire extinguisher. Your vehicle also needs to have headlamp deflectors. The speed limit in Greece is 130km per hour on freeways and 50km an hour on urban roads. The alcohol limit in Greece is under 0.5 g/l. Children under the age of 10 are not allowed to ride in the front seat. It is illegal to use your mobile phone while driving.

🌐 Smoking Laws

Greece is the European country with the highest tobacco consumption rate. As a result, the population has been very tolerant of smoking, even with the introduction of anti-smoking legislation. In fact, business owners have appealed against various forms of anti-smoking laws, arguing that they are bad for business. Smoking in public places has been banned since 2010, but the law provides for bars, taverns, casinos, night clubs and betting shops to create a designated smoking area. It is also illegal to smoke in your car, if in the company of a minor child.

🌐 Drinking Laws

The legal drinking age in Greece is 18. Although Greece has a culture of social drinking, bars and night clubs may state that alcohol will not be served to under 18s or even, in the case of certain cruise tours, under 21s. Alcohol can be bought from supermarkets and even fast food outlets.

🌐 Electricity

Electricity: 230 volts

Frequency: 50 Hz

Greek electricity sockets use the Type F plugs, which feature two round pins or prongs. They are also compatible with Type C and Type E plugs. If travelling from the USA, you will need a power converter or transformer to convert the voltage from 230 to 110, to avoid damage to your appliances. The latest models of many laptops, camcorders, mobile phones and digital cameras are dual-voltage with a built in converter.

🌐 Tourist Information (TI)

There are three National Tourist Offices in the city of Athens where you can pick up maps of the city, as well as time tables for the Greek bus, train and ferry services. They are located at Athens Eleftherios Venizelos Airport, in the Athens Center at 26A Amalias Avenue and 7 Tsoha Street.

🌐 Food & Drink

Greek cuisine relies heavily on the use of olive oil (and olives), cheese and aubergines (or eggplant). Beef is rare, but there are plenty of lamb and pork dishes to make up for it. One of the most popular Greek dishes is moussaka, a casserole consisting

MYKONOS TRAVEL GUIDE

of layers of eggplant and spiced mince. Try the baked pasta dish, pastitsio or if you like meat stews, do make sure that you try stifado as well. With an abundance of seafood available, don't forget to enjoy the abundance of grilled fish and octopus. A course of small meze dishes is often served as appetizer or to accompany a round of drinks. The standard meze favorites include tzatziki (a dip of yoghurt and cucumber), hummus (made of chickpea), dolmades, keftedes, olives, feta cheese and taramasalata (a fish roe dip), usually served with pita or flatbread. Another delicious appetizer is saganaki, or fried cheese, often made with halloumi, kefalotyri, graviera, kefalograviera or feta. Graviera, which is a native product of Crete, is the second most popular cheese in Greece after feta. Fast and meaty snacks to enjoy on the go are souvlaki (meat skewers), kebabs or gyros - pitas filed with meat, French fries and smothered in tzatziki. Phyllo pastry is used for a variety of dishes, including the standard dessert of baklava and tiropitakia (or cheese pies). If you happen to find yourself on Mykonos, do make sure you sample kopanisti, a cheesy appetizer, a few slices of louza, the local salami and some amigthalota, to indulge your sweet tooth. Crete is a must for cheese lovers, where practically every village has its own distinctive varieties. Here you can also enjoy Askordoulakous or "mountain bulbs", lamb with stamnagathi or sfakia pies. For a taste of manouri - a cheese similar to feta with a creamier character - you need to be in Thessaly or Macedonia.

MYKONOS TRAVEL GUIDE

The most popular beers local beer in Greece is Mythos, although Amstel and Heineken are also available at most venues. Retsina is the type of wine most often associated with Greece, although its distinctive taste of resin is not all that popular with foreigners. Another popular drink is ouzo, a strong liquor with a minty taste that combines well with seafood. If visiting Epirus, Macedonia or Crete, to sample the local raki and tsipouro, which is served in small shot glasses. If you want to quench your thirst with something refreshing and non-alcoholic, try soumada, a Cretan beverage of almond and rose water.

Websites

http://www.visitgreece.gr/

http://www.greeka.com/best-greece-destinations.htm

http://www.greek-tourism.gr/

http://wikitravel.org/en/Greece

http://www.visit-ancient-greece.com/

http://www.greektravel.com/mainland.htm

Printed in Great Britain
by Amazon